CONTENTS

I0886052

FOLLOW THE MERMAID

The round, green-and-white Starbucks® **logo** is everywhere. It shows a mermaid with two tails. The design has been through many changes over more than 50 years. But the mermaid has always been there.

People around the world recognize the symbol. The company doesn't even put the name *Starbucks* on it anymore. Everyone knows that the mermaid means coffee.

Starbucks is known for more than just coffee. The company wants people to think of its shops as a "third place." That's a warm and welcoming place to relax that is not home or work.

Tables at Starbucks are full of people talking. Friends sip **lattes** and chat. Small business owners meet clients. You might overhear people planning a wedding. Students do homework together.

THE LAUNCH OF STARBUCKS

Starbucks began in 1971 in Seattle, Washington. Three coffee-loving friends decided to start a business. They each gave 1,350 dollars. They also borrowed 5,000 dollars.

The three friends named their company Starbucks. That's the name of a character in the famous novel about a giant whale, *Moby-Dick*. The **founders** also designed a mermaid logo. The ocean-related name and sign connected with the coastal city of Seattle.

At first, Starbucks was just one shop in the famous public market in Seattle called Pike Place Market. The shop sold coffee beans, teas, and spices. It didn't sell prepared drinks.

Starbucks at Pike Place today

Starbucks Shorts

The first store had just one paid employee. That was Zev Siegl, one of the three founders.

Starbucks grew to four Seattle **franchises**. Howard Schultz joined the company in 1982. He loved the coffee **cafés** he had visited in Italy. He saw how they were lively places where people could gather and connect. He wanted Starbucks to be like them.

But the original Starbucks founders viewed coffee as an art. They loved creating new blends of coffee beans. They didn't want Starbucks to become a restaurant that served coffee.

Schultz left Starbucks in 1985. Then, two years later, he bought the whole company. Soon after, the Starbucks stores became coffeehouses. Using this **business model**, Schultz guided the company to worldwide coffee fame

Howard Schultz

MAKE YOURSELF COMFORTABLE

A typical Starbucks location has a welcoming feel. Dark wooden tables and cozy chairs await. Photos of coffee farms line the walls. Soft lighting creates a friendly mood.

Different franchises reflect their neighborhoods. A southern Florida location is decorated with palm frond patterns. A Utah location has glass walls that showcase nearby mountains.

Dubai

Paris, France

Starbucks Shorts

A Starbucks in Paris, France, has fancy chandeliers and murals on the ceiling.

Customers go up to the counter to order. The **barista** will ask for lots of information about the drink you want. What size: short, tall, grande, or venti? Hot or iced? Whole milk, skim milk, or nondairy milk? What flavor of syrup? When they've got all the details, a worker will use a marker to write your name on your cup.

Starbucks Shorts

Some customers sound like they're speaking a made-up language. You might hear, "Iced double tall mocha, extra whip" or "Blonde flat white with half caramel syrup, half vanilla." It's all coffee talk.

You can pick up your drink at the far end of the counter. Then, settle into a cushy chair or find a table. The buzz of conversation will surround you. The coffee machines will hiss and clank. The blender will roar. It will all fade into the background as you read, relax, or chat.

DRINK IT IN

Starbucks is the world's most popular coffeehouse. There are lots of items on the menu, including food, but coffee is the star. Many people love rich, dark, hot coffee. Some folks drink iced coffee, especially on hot days.

Starbucks drinks often combine coffee with other ingredients. A latte has extra-strong coffee, steamed milk, and milk foam. A Frappuccino® is milk, coffee, and flavored syrups blended with ice. Whipped cream and candy might top it off.

Starbucks Shorts

Customers can order their drinks "upside-down." That just means the ingredients will be poured into the cup in reverse order.

PSL

Starbucks is a master of seasonal flavors. Its all-time bestseller is the pumpkin spice latte, which is only available in the fall. Since the PSL was introduced in 2003, people have bought hundreds of millions of the cinnamony drinks.

EGGNOG LATTE

PEPPERMINT MOCHA

Flavors like eggnog and peppermint show up during the winter. In spring, lavender pops up on the menu. Customers rush to buy drinks available for only a short time.

Some non-coffee drinks are also wildly popular. **Concoctions** like the Pink Drink Refresher or the Matcha Crème Frappuccino blend fruit juices, lemonade, tea, hot chocolate, and other ingredients.

PINK DRINK REFRESHER

Starbucks Shorts

The Unicorn Frappuccino was available for just five days in 2017. The color-changing drink contained mango syrup and a sour blue drizzle.

Starbucks buys coffee grown in more than 30 countries, including China, Costa Rica, and Ethiopia. Coffee beans grown in different places have different flavors. Soil and weather affect the flavor.

Starbucks says that their coffee is 99 percent **ethically sourced**. That means farmers are paid fairly and use methods that don't harm the planet. But some groups argue that Starbucks buys coffee from farms that treat their workers poorly. Starbucks must solve problems like this so customers can trust them.

Starbucks Shorts

Costa Rica has many volcanoes. The eruptions affect the soil there. The minerals in volcanic soil make it great for growing coffee.

STARBUCKS IN OUR WORLD

Starbucks uses ads and marketing campaigns to entice people to visit its stores. These include **collaborations** with celebrities, or collabs for short.

Every year, Starbucks has a special red holiday cup. In 2021, Taylor Swift's album was called *Red (Taylor's Version)*. So, Starbucks added Taylor's Latte to their menu.

Starbucks has also named drinks after Ariana Grande and Oprah Winfrey. It hopes that a celebrity's fans will become Starbucks fans too.

Taylor Swift

Starbucks Shorts

Nutrition experts warn people to stop and think before a clever ad persuades them to order a fancy Starbucks drink. A Cloud Macchiato, the drink inspired by Ariana Grande, can contain a whopping 27 grams of sugar.

In 1997, the Starbucks Foundation began supporting reading education programs. The charity helps many people learn job skills. It has worked with military veterans, people with disabilities, and young adults who aren't in school.

Other Starbucks Foundation efforts support clean water and schools in coffee-growing regions. It's invested more than 25 million dollars to these causes since 2005.

Starbucks Shorts

Starbucks lets customers bring and use their own coffee cups. It was the first national coffeehouse chain to do this. The practice helps fight waste and pollution.

STARBUCKS

With its delicious coffee drinks and other menu items, the company with the familiar mermaid logo has become a mega-success around the world. Customers spend more than 36 billion dollars each year at Starbucks.

There are over 38,000 Starbucks franchises in more than 80 countries. The company employs nearly 400,000 workers. This big business has a big influence on our culture and our world.

Starbucks Shorts

Starbucks calls its employees partners. Many partners feel they are not paid enough and do not have enough say in how the company is run.

A STARBUCKS TIME LINE

1971 Three friends open the first Starbucks shop in Seattle, Washington.

1982 The fifth Starbucks location opens. Howard Schultz joins the company. He wants to focus on running coffeehouses.

1985 Schultz leaves the company.

1987 Schultz buys Starbucks.

1995 Frappuccino blended beverages join the menu.

1996 The first Starbucks outside North America opens, in Japan.

1997 The Starbucks Foundation is established.

2003 The Pumpkin Spice Latte (PSL) appears on the menu.

2009 Starbucks begins its loyalty program for repeat customers.

2018 Schultz retires from the company.

2020 Strawless lids are introduced to reduce the use of plastic straws and help the planet.

2021 Starbucks workers vote to establish a labor union in Buffalo, New York.

2024 Summer Berry Refreshers, with flavored pearls in each cup, are introduced.

Starbucks headquarters in Seattle, WA

GLOSSARY

barista (buh-REE-stuh)
a person who makes and serves coffee

business model (BIZ-nis MAH-duhl)
a plan or design for selling a company's products

cafés (ka-FAYZ)
small restaurants that serve light meals and drinks

collaborations (kuh-la-buh-RAY-shuhnz)
partnerships or joint projects

concoctions (kuhn-KAHKT-shuhnz)
mixtures made by combining different ingredients

ethically sourced (E-thi-kuh-lee sorsd)
gotten from makers or sellers who use fair practices and who treat employees well

founders (FOUN-durz)
the people who start a company or organization

franchises (fran-CHYE-sis)
individual locations of a chain store or restaurant; legal agreements that let people run businesses that sell products created by a larger company

lattes (LAH-tayz)
drinks made from very strong coffee and steamed milk

logo (LOH-goh)
a symbol that identifies a company

FACT CHECK

1. The Starbucks name and logo both connect to _____.
   A. the sea B. money C. coffee

2. Starbucks did not sell _____ when it first opened.
   A. hot coffee B. teas C. spices

3. The city where Starbucks started is _____.
   A. San Antonio, Texas B. Chicago, Illinois
   C. Seattle, Washington

4. The coffee beans Starbucks uses come from _____.
   A. Africa B. more than 30 countries C. just Costa Rica

Answers: 1. A, 2. A, 3. C, 4. B

FURTHER READING

Cohn, Jessica. *On the Job in a Restaurant*. South Egremont, MA: Red Chair Press, 2016.

Kids in the Kitchen. *Chef in Training: 100+ Easy & Yummy Recipes with Cooking Tips*. New York: Kitchen Ink Publishing, 2023.

Kittleson, Neil, and the Great Coffee Project. *Andy Visits a Coffee Farm*. Baltimore, MD: The Great Coffee Project, 2022.

ON THE INTERNET

Biz Kid$: Young Entrepreneur Profiles
https://bizkids.com/groups/profiles
Learn about young people who have started their own companies.

Food Network: Cooking with Kids
https://www.foodnetwork.com/recipes/packages/recipes-for-kids/cooking-with-kids
Find recipes from the network for fun in the kitchen.

National Coffee Association: 10 Steps from Seed to Cup
https://www.ncausa.org/About-Coffee/10-Steps-from-Seed-to-Cup
See how coffee goes from a seed to a popular drink.

INDEX

ABOUT THE AUTHOR

Laura Purdie Salas is an award-winning author who lives and writes in Minnesota. Her many books include poetry and nonfiction. Laura loves to read, play board games, knit, explore nature, and spend time with her husband and two daughters. She also eats way too much fast food! Her favorite Starbucks menu item is a hot chocolate with extra whipped cream. Visit Laura at laurasalas.com.